Growing
Through
Arts!™

by Aleksandra ℠

THE
Sleeping Beauty
BALLET

BY Aleksandra SM

BALLET SERIES

ORCHID PUBLISHING | CHICAGO

Director of Publications
Orchid Publishing, Inc.
333 N. Michigan Ave., #222
Chicago, IL 60601
www.orchid-publishing.com

Illustrations by Elizaveta Efimova

Special Thanks to Russian Pointe Dance Boutique, Joffrey Ballet, Scott Speck, Auditorium Theatre of Roosevelt
University, River North Dance Company and Vala Dancewear for Glossary photos.

Library of Congress Control Number: 2010918294
ISBN 978-0-9831641-2-8

Production Date: January 20, 2011
Printing Plant Location: Everbest Printing Co. Ltd.,
    Nansha, China
Job/Batch #: EPC-RN-97951.4 R4

We never forget the moment we first set foot in a place that takes our breath away!
I remember seeing the Mariinsky Theatre, home of the Kirov Ballet, for the first time. I was
transported to a whole new world! Everything I laid my eyes on—the stage, the curtains,
the orchestra, the set decorations, the costumes—made me want to learn more.

There was so much to discover and understand!

I now invite you to turn the page and embark on the captivating story of *Sleeping Beauty*.

As with our previous two stories, this one celebrates the art of ballet and also presents new
ballet vocabulary words and character-building principles you'll want your child to embrace.

May it serve as an inspiration for creative discovery and endless learning!

I hope this book helps your child confidently build a life of fulfillment,
just as *Sleeping Beauty* does.

Ever Growing Through Arts,
Aleksandra

How to Use This Book

- Read the story to your child many times to encourage memory and to explore the themes more deeply.

- Pretend you're in a theater, watching the "ballet" unfold on stage!

- Read and discuss **Miss Aleksandra's Themes & Values**, integrated throughout the book, and look for ways to relate them to your child's life.

- At the end of the book, use **Miss Aleksandra's Glossary** to learn the new vocabulary words introduced in the story and to enjoy beautiful photo illustrations of ballet concepts.

- Engage in a thoughtful dialogue with your child—ask questions about the story, pictures, and characters.

- Expand your fun and learning time with your child by doing activities in the **Practice & Play** book (sold separately), which integrates characters and story elements from the storybook.

It's **opening night** for the ballet *Sleeping Beauty*! Shhh. The audience hushes as the **orchestra** plays the first notes of Tchaikovsky's **score**. The dancers finish putting on **makeup**, hurry to their places, and wait for the curtain to rise. They are eager to tell this timeless tale of love and magic . . .

Deep in the Fairy Forest, in the castle of a king, a princess named Aurora was born. The Queen and King loved their baby girl very much and wanted to share their joy with everyone. They decided to hold a party.

The whole kingdom was invited, along with all of the forest fairies. Well, *almost* all. There was one fairy the King and Queen did not invite.

Carabosse, the Wicked Fairy.

Is it all right to leave one person out of your party if you don't like that person? What do you think?

8

The Wicked Fairy was true to her name. She treated everyone like an enemy and spent her days conjuring curses.

When she learned of the Princess's party, she thundered, "Why was I not invited?" and hurled a fireball into a tree. "WHYYYY?"

MISS Aleksandra's
THEMES &
VALUES

If you treat someone like an enemy, how do you think that person might treat you?

On the evening of the party, the King and Queen greeted their guests. The last to arrive was a beautiful fairy no one had seen before. She wore a sparkling **leotard** and shimmering slippers.

"We do not know you," said the King, "but please be our welcome guest."

The beautiful fairy slid her foot forward in a graceful **tendu**, then danced lightly across the ballroom floor. When all eyes were upon her, she performed a perfect **plié**.

Then she tore off her wig and revealed her true form: Carabosse. "Why was I not invited?" she shrieked.

"I'm very sorry," said the Queen. "Please accept our apology."

"Never!" shouted Carabosse. "But I do have a lovely gift for your baby— a CURSE! On her eighteenth birthday, Aurora will prick her finger and breathe no more!"

The Wicked Fairy vanished in a puff of smoke.

MISS *Aleksandra's* THEMES & VALUES

It's important to accept an apology when it's offered. Carabosse takes revenge instead. What do you think about that?

12

Aurora's parents felt stabbed with grief.
"Fear not," spoke the Lilac Fairy.
"I, too, have a gift for Aurora.
I will give it on her
eighteenth birthday!"

The years passed and the King and Queen forgot about the Wicked Fairy's curse. Aurora made it easy to forget bad things. She was a fearless girl, full of love and joy. She loved the wind, the trees, and the creatures of the forest. She treated everyone like a friend.

Aurora **expressed** herself beautifully in everything she did. Because she had no fear in her heart, she danced like an angel, sang like a songbird, and painted pictures that shone like jewels.

MISS
Aleksandra's
THEMES &
VALUES

When we express ourselves without fear, our natural talents come to life!

Her love was so great that all things she wanted came easily to her.
Except for one—a young man to love.

As Aurora grew older she began to dream about her first kiss. "I know the man I will truly love," she told her bluebird friends. "He is strong but never hurts anyone. He is brave but doesn't boast. He is a lover of the forest and a lover of beauty."

But Aurora could not find such a young man anywhere.

MISS *Aleksandra's* THEMES & VALUES

A positive, loving attitude invites wonderful things into your life.

Her parents decided to hold a ball for her eighteenth birthday. They made sure to invite all the young men in the kingdom.

The Birthday Ball was spectacular. The best part of all was Aurora's dance. From her very first **relevé** she held the audience spellbound.

All of the young men fought for her attention. But the more they brawled and bragged, the less interested Aurora was. She knew her true love would not act this way.

Finally, the last guest arrived—a kindly seamstress, carrying a tapestry. "May I give this to Aurora?" she asked.

As the seamstress drew near to her, Aurora had a strange feeling. It seemed the woman was only **miming** an expression of kindness. The moment Aurora took the tapestry, a hidden pin pricked her finger!

The seamstress was really Carabosse, the Wicked Fairy! "Perhaps you forgot my curse," she told the King and Queen, "but I did not. Say goodbye to your daughter, for she dies today!" And Carabosse vanished.

Just then the Lilac Fairy appeared. "I promised Aurora a gift on this special birthday," she said. "My gift is this: "Aurora will not die, she will only sleep."

"Oh, thank you, thank you!" cried the Queen.

"But be warned," said the fairy. "She will sleep for a very long time and can only be awakened by true love's kiss."

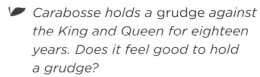

Carabosse holds a grudge *against the King and Queen for eighteen years. Does it feel good to hold a grudge?*

The Lilac Fairy keeps a promise *she made eighteen years ago. Does it feel good to keep a promise?*

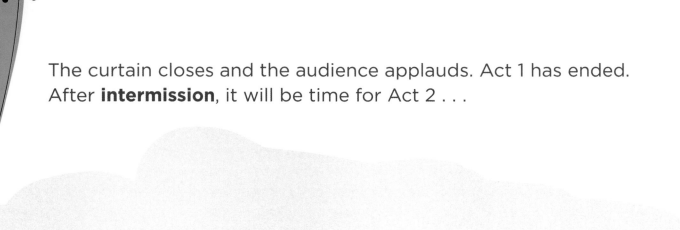

The curtain closes and the audience applauds. Act 1 has ended.
After **intermission**, it will be time for Act 2 . . .

A *hundred years* passed and Aurora lay in her bed,
unable to move. But she had found a peaceful
place inside her where time disappeared.
From that place, she called out
silently to her true love . . .

*Learning to be still and quiet can
bring you a beautiful feeling of
peace. Many artists are inspired
by spending time in silence.*

One day, a handsome prince named Florimund was hiking through the woods with his hunting party. "When do we start shooting?" asked his friend.

"We don't," said the prince. "I want to *paint* the animals, not shoot them."

"Brave Prince Florimund," teased the friend. "Hunts with a paintbrush instead of a bow. Bet the ladies love that!"

The prince felt hurt by his friend's words and wanted to be alone. "I'll meet you later," he told the others.

Some people think boys need to act rough and tough in order to be brave and strong. What do you think?

Florimund wandered off by himself, letting the quiet of the forest soothe his mood. "Tell me, little friend," he said to a bluebird, "is there a woman alive who can love a man like me? One who likes beauty more than hunting and fighting?"

The bluebird fluttered off. As the prince turned to watch
it go, he spotted a castle tower covered in vines! It
looked as if no one had entered it in a hundred years.
It seemed to call to his heart.

The prince climbed the vines with great strength and jumped through the window. Lying there asleep was the most beautiful woman he'd ever seen.

He took a step closer.

Carabosse appeared before him, wearing her most frightful face!
"You will not kiss her and spoil my curse!" she roared.

But the prince was not afraid. He looked calmly into the wicked
fairy's eyes and said only the words, "Step aside." So pure was his
courage that the fairy lost her power and shrank into a harmless
old woman. 🍂

🍂 *When someone yells at you, should you yell back or speak calmly?*
Can you be brave without shouting or fighting?

The prince gazed at Aurora and his heart melted with love. He leaned over and kissed her lips. Aurora awakened! Her parents awakened, too, for the Lilac Fairy had let them sleep along with Aurora.

Aurora took one look at Florimund and knew she had found true love.

26

"Go ahead and kill me now," growled Carabosse. "I know you want to."

"I wish you no harm," said Florimund. "You harm *yourself* with your unkind thoughts and actions."

"Go and be happy," Aurora told her. "We forgive you."

No one had ever spoken to Carabosse with kindness. She felt love in her heart for the very first time. It spread like warm butter from the top of her head to the tips of her toes. She touched Aurora's hand and wept.

Florimund is very wise. He knows that people who hold grudges hurt themselves more than anyone else

Have you ever forgiven someone? How did it feel? Has anyone ever forgiven you? Forgiveness makes two people feel better!.

Aurora and Florimund were
married in a glorious ceremony.
Their special guest was Carabosse,
the Kind Fairy.

And when their daughter was born she had the most *wonderful* fairy godmother. And they all lived together in love and happiness.

The curtain closes and the audience gives the dancers a **standing ovation**! That's all for now. But soon there will be another performance.

Love and forgiveness have amazing power to change people.

Glossary

MISS *Aleksandra's* GLOSSARY

COURTESY JOFFREY BALLET

expression

To use **expression** in dance means to bring out feeling or character by the *way* the movements are performed. *Expression* in any kind of art means showing feelings in a special and personal way.

Intermission is the time between acts in a ballet. During intermission the audience can stretch or enjoy a snack while the performers get ready for the next act.

A **leotard** is a tight-fitting outfit worn by dancers.

COURTESY VALA DANCEWEAR

leotard

Dancers put on **makeup** to help them look like their story characters. Makeup also helps the audience to see the dancers' faces under bright stage lights.

To **mime** means to *express* a feeling or action by using the face and the body.

Opening night is the first performance of a ballet by a dance company.

The **orchestra** is made up of musicians who play the music for the ballet.

When doing a **plié**, a dancer gracefully bends both knees away from one another.

make up

mime

orchestra

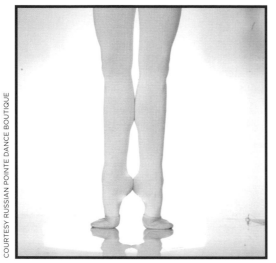

relevé

standing ovation

To do a **relevé**, the dancer lifts up onto the balls of the feet.

The **score** is the music that a composer writes for a ballet.

When audience members stand on their feet to applaud a wonderful performance, it's called a **standing ovation**.

A **tendu** is a step in which the dancer stretches out a foot, but the foot does not leave the floor.

ABOUT *Aleksandra* SM

Aleksandra Efimova is the founder of **Growing Through Arts**™ and President of Russian Pointe, Inc., a brand of luxury ballet shoes with a flagship boutique on Chicago's Magnificent Mile. Born in St. Petersburg, Russia, Aleksandra graduated from the renowned Art School at the Hermitage State Art Museum and received training in classical dance, art, and academics. In 1993, she moved to United States, where she started her first successful company while still an undergraduate student. An alumna of Harvard Business School, she is an inspirational speaker and writer and is actively involved in promoting the arts, international collaboration, and education in the community.

OTHER BOOKS IN
THE GROWING THROUGH ARTS™

BALLET SERIES

The Nutcracker Ballet by Aleksandra^{SM} (storybook)

The Cinderella Ballet by Aleksandra^{SM} (storybook)

The Nutcracker Ballet Practice & Play Book by Aleksandra^{SM}

The Cinderella Ballet Practice & Play Book by Aleksandra^{SM}

The Sleeping Beauty Ballet Practice & Play Book by Aleksandra^{SM}

MUSIC SERIES

The Peter and the Wolf Symphony by Aleksandra^{SM} (storybook)

The Snow Maiden Opera by Aleksandra^{SM} (storybook)

Twist, A Musical by Aleksandra^{SM} (storybook)

The Peter and the Wolf Symphony Practice & Play Book by Aleksandra^{SM}

The Snow Maiden Opera Practice & Play Book by Aleksandra^{SM}

Twist, A Musical Practice & Play Book by Aleksandra^{SM}

hrough Art, Gro
Gro

rough Art

Growing Thro